PAPIER MÂCHÉ

By SUSAN MOXLEY AND JULIET BAWDEN

Written by Juliet Bawden and Orine James

Photography by Jon Barnes

CONTENTS

EQUIPMENT

Papier mâché comes from a French word meaning 'chewed paper'. It is made by building up layers of paper and paste over a mould. When the paste dries, the paper is quite firm and can be painted and varnished.

You do not need any special equipment or tools to make papier mâché, but all of the things shown here are useful.

Newspaper is particularly good for making papier mâché but old wrapping paper or tissue paper can be used. You can use wallpaper paste following the instructions on the packet or make your own paste using the recipe on the next page.

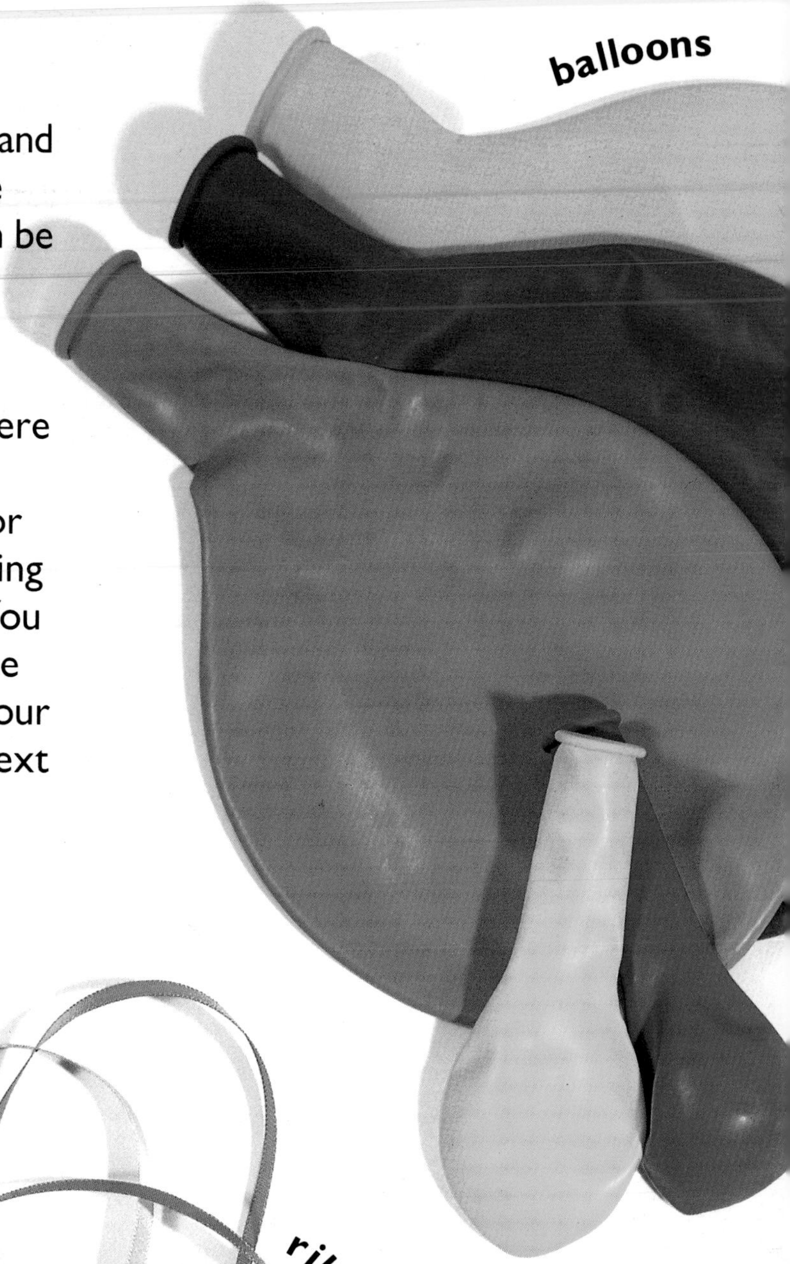

balloons

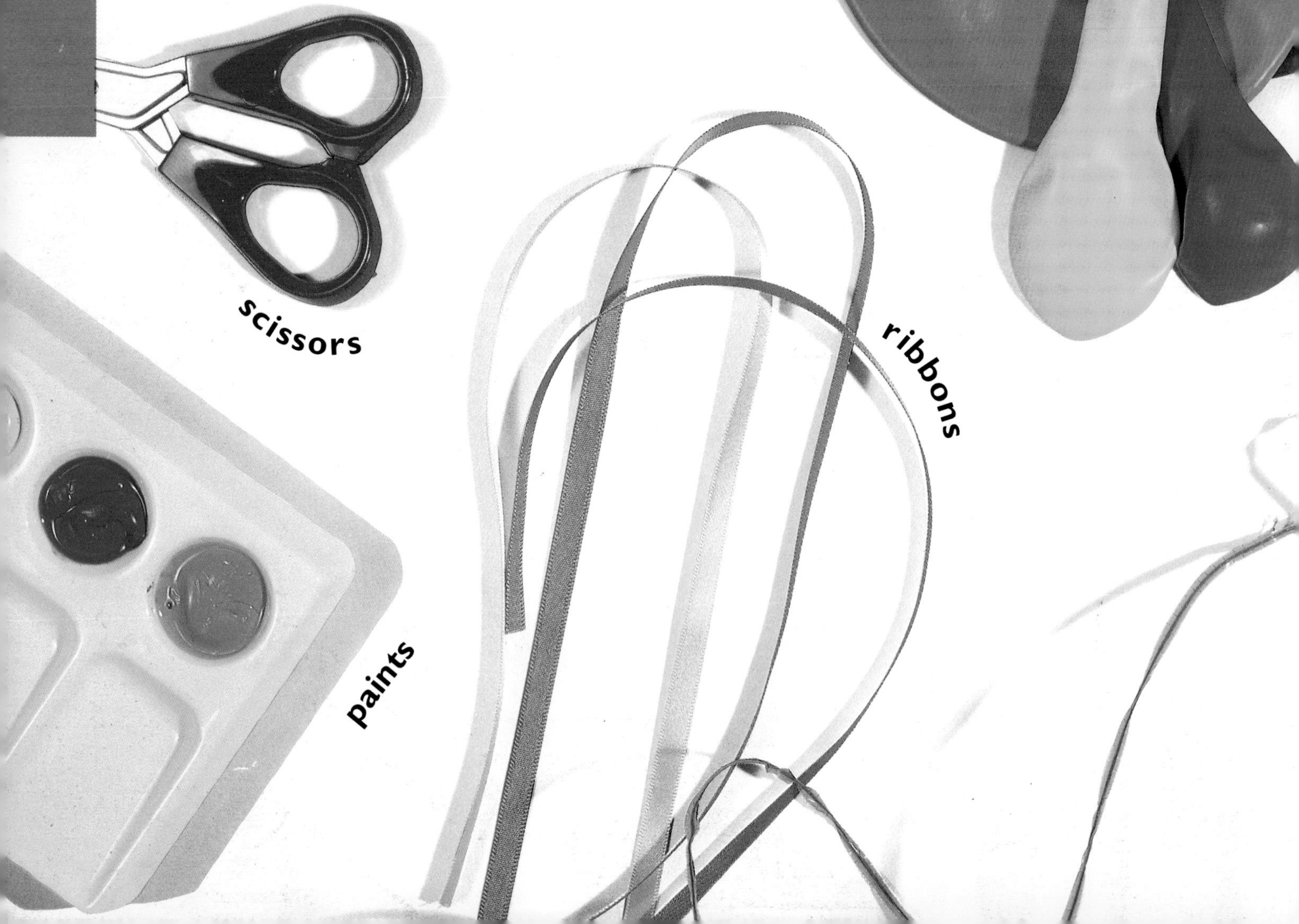

scissors

ribbons

paints

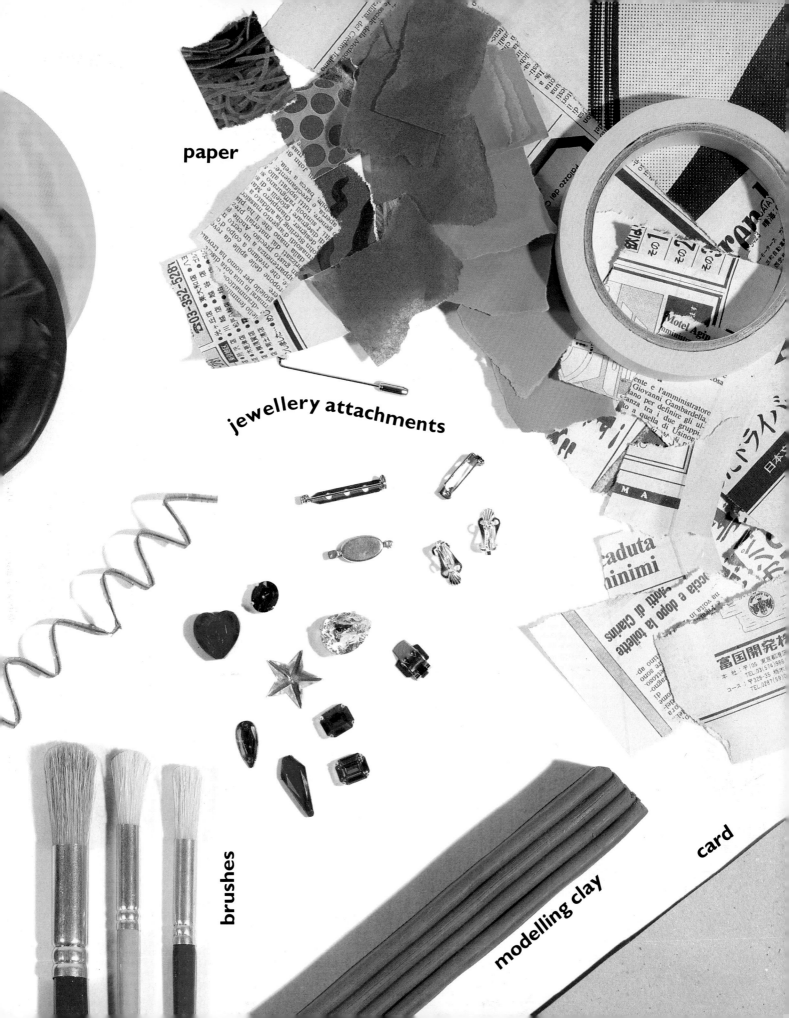

paper

jewellery attachments

brushes

modelling clay

card

There are two methods for making papier mâché. The first is called *layering*, where paste or PVA glue is spread on to strips of paper and several layers are built up over a mould. The second uses *pulp*. This can be used in the same way as modelling clay for making small shapes.

Making Pulp

Fill a bucket with paper torn into 25mm squares. Pour enough warm water over the paper to cover it and leave to soak for 24 hours. Strain off the water and add paste or PVA glue gradually until the pulp feels like soft clay.

Wallpaper Paste

Mix according to the instructions on the packet, adding the powder gradually to warm water until it is completely dissolved.

wallpaper paste

pulp

Home-Made Paste

Measure out one mug of flour and three mugs of water. In a saucepan, mix the flour with a little of the water to make a smooth paste. Add the rest of the water and ask a grown-up to heat the mixture until it boils, stirring all the time! Turn the heat down and simmer until the paste thickens. Leave the mixture until it is cold.

Layering

You can rip paper into long strips and spread paste on to each strip as you work. Or, spread the paste on to a large sheet of paper. Rip the paper in half lengthways. Stick one piece on top of the other so that both pieces are glue side up. Repeat so you have four layers. Paste these over your mould.

layering

home-made paste

You can make bowls, vases and jugs by using moulds such as balloons, large bottles and cake tins. First, cover the mould with oil or Vaseline so you can pull the papier mâché object off easily when it is finished. You will need at least six layers of papier mâché to make a firm shape. Let it dry throughly before taking off the mould. This may take two or three days.

Leave the rim uneven or neaten it off by gluing overlapping strips of paper round it. You can also trim the edge by carefully cutting round it with scissors.

You can make handles and lids
afterwards by adding strips of card
and covering them with papier
mâché. Try decorating a bowl with
pulp shapes.

When your papier mâché objects are completely dry –
usually after two to three days – you can decorate them
with paint or coloured paper. If you have used
newspaper, it is a good idea to cover the object with a
base coat of white emulsion paint.

After you have decorated the papier mâché, you can
protect it with a final coat of varnish. Watered-down
PVA can also be used. If you want your papier mâché to
be waterproof, use two or three layers of varnish.

To make a circular bowl stand up, you will have to
give it a base. The bowl above has conical feet made
by taping card cones to the bowl before decorating.

Here are some toys to make from papier mâché. We made the cat using a washing liquid bottle as a mould. For the others, we made our own moulds using a small balloon, wire, card and a pair of tights for stuffing! Try making a simple shape from card, paper and sticky tape. Cover your shape with layers of papier mâché. It does not matter if you cannot remove the finished papier mâché shape from the mould.

Bird

Crumple a large ball of paper for the body. Make a card roll for the neck and a ball of paper for the head. Add a small card cone for the beak. Tape wire legs to the body. Cover the whole bird in layers of papier mâché. When it is dry, paint in bright colours.

Russian Dolls

Start with a mould made from an egg-shaped piece of modelling clay. Cover with layers of papier mâché. When the papier mâché is dry, cut through three-quarters of the way up. To make the two pieces stay together, make a ring from a thin strip of card and tape it inside the bottom half. Make lots of different-sized dolls to fit inside one another.

Fish

Cut out two fish shapes from card. Staple the shapes together leaving a gap to stuff with crumpled paper. Cover with layers of papier mâché. Paint the fish when the papier mâché is dry.

Teddy Bears

Look for small cake or jelly moulds. Cover them with a layer of Vaseline and then with layers of papier mâché. Paint when dry.

All of this wonderful jewellery is made from papier mâché! The golden 'jewels' were made from paper pulp. You can buy jewellery fittings, such as brooch backs and earring clips, from craft shops.

Bows

Paste several strips of newspaper together and fold each end into the middle to make a bow shape. Paste a thin strip of paper round the middle of the bow.

Earrings

Cut shapes from card and tape on some crumpled paper to act as padding. Cover the card and paper with layers of paste and paper. Decorate your earrings and glue on earring backs.

Beads

You can make simple beads by winding strips of pasted paper round a straw or pencil. Leave to dry before decorating and threading them. Beads can also be made from pulp (see recipe on page 4). Mould the pulp into shapes and make a hole with a knitting needle. Or, push in paper clips to make links.

Bangles

Look out for cardboard tubes
that you can cut down to make
bases. Or, use strips of card
glued into a circle. Use tissue
paper as padding and cover with
strips of pasted paper.
Try decorating your bangles with
strips of coloured paper.

You can even make exotic hats with papier mâché! Round cake tins make good moulds for simple hats. Or, you could use a balloon to make a rounded top and add a cardboard brim.

Try decorating your hats with papier mâché flowers and animals. Or, use paper pulp to make brightly coloured jewels.

Believe it or not, you can make music from papier mâché! By using simple hollow moulds and moulds filled with dry beans, you can start your own band.

Drum

Use a cake tin as a mould, and make two papier mâché sections like the ones here. Cut two holes in the top section and thread some cord through. Join the sections together with strips of pasted paper. When the drum is dry, decorate it with bright colours.

Tambourine

Make a band from card and cut four wide slits round it. Thread beads, washers or bottle tops on to cocktail sticks and tape the sticks to the middle of each slit. Cover with layers of papier mâché and decorate.

Maracas

Cover a small balloon with papier mâché, leaving a hole at one end. Fill with dried peas or beans. Add a handle and decorate.

Papier mâché has been used for hundreds of years to make puppets. Countries all over the world have their own traditional designs.

Try making glove, string or finger puppets from papier mâché. You will find some helpful hints on the next page. You could also make a simple stage and hold your own puppet show!

Glove Puppet

Make a simple head shape from crumpled paper. Attach it to a neck made from a circle of card. Add features such as ears and noses and cover with papier mâché. Paint on other features when the head is dry.

Cut two rectangles from pieces of fabric and stitch together to make the body. Remember to leave holes for your fingers and a hole to push the card tube through. Decorate with ribbons, buttons or beads.

Finger Puppets

Make a roll of card to fit round your finger. You can add details, such as a head made from crumpled paper, or beaks and ears made from card cones or a hat with a brim. Cover the shape with papier mâché and decorate it when it is dry. Try making a different puppet for each finger.

Spoon Puppet

Wrap layers of paper round the top of a wooden spoon to make a head shape. Cover with layers of papier mâché. Tie a length of dowel under the head to make a 'T' shape. Make the body by sewing two rectangles of fabric together and fitting over the 'T' shape.

Masks are great fun for parties, especially if you don't want anyone to recognise you! You can make exciting masks from papier mâché, and they can be used over and over again.

Many countries have traditional masks that are worn for festivals. You may be able to find inspiration by looking at these in books and museums.

One of the simplest ways to make a mask is to cover half a balloon with papier mâché. You can add cardboard cones, sections from packaging, or pieces of crumpled paper to make extra features.

Make holes on either side of the mask and attach string or ribbons to tie round your head. Don't forget to make holes for the eyes.